I0554905

Iaroslav Wise

The Brief Methodological Notes For Church School Instructors

The purpose of this book is not to provide a step by step guide for establishing a Church school or to give a set of lesson plans, but to help instructors and other Church school volunteers align on the key point of departure (well begun is half done) and to serve as a quick reference for the things that are frequently used at a Church school, such as prayers before a meal and before a lesson, carols, feast and fast dates, Church greetings and more.

Wise, I. (2023). *Brief Methodological Notes For Church School Instructors*. Calgary, AB: Edocation Corp.

ISBN 978-1-989531-43-3

Format: book (paperback)
Languages: English, Ukrainian
Written & designed by: Iaroslav Wise
Published by: Edocation Corp.
Disclaimer: this book is published as has been submitted by the author and in the original languages

TABLE OF CONTENTS

INTRODUCTION

> "You shall love the Lord your God with all your heart, with all your soul, and with all your mind. (...) You shall love your neighbour as yourself"
>
> *(Mt 22:37; 39)*.

These are the two greatest commandments around which a true Christian life is built in its every aspect. Therefore, these are also the commandments which should power education at Church schools. These commandments are to be practised and students are to be instructed in them. Those Church schools that stick to these and do so cheerfully can stay assured that the key objective of their curriculum has been achieved successfully and all other things will follow.

The purpose of this book is not to provide a step by step guide for creating a Church school or a set of lessons, but rather to help align on the key point of departure (well begun is half done) and to serve as a quick reference for the things that are frequently used at a Church school (e.g. instructors and students can read the prayers before a lesson from it).

The book is divided into two parts. The first one discusses the questions that are specific to Church schools and that are often assumed, but not always articulated (e.g. why to attend a Church school, why to volunteer, which resources to use, etc.). The other part focuses on general Church-related matters, such as a brief history, carols, Church greetings and more. This book is written for Ukrainian Orthodox Church schools in Canada, but it may be useful to other Church schools in Canada and beyond.

THE SCHOOL
A Note to the Instructor

> "For God has not given us a spirit of fear, but of power and of love and of a sound mind" (*2Tim 1:7*).

Dear Instructor,

The Lord has entrusted you with the most precious part of the Church, her present and future – the youngest members of the congregation. Not much is required of you to fulfill this calling duly: to be a true Orthodox Christian and be an example to the students, just as Christ is to all of us, and to explain the things pertinent to our faith to your students in plain terms and without haste, with abundant examples and gratitude to God for all.

In this, you are not alone. The Lord, in Whom you trust, is able to give you wisdom and everything that you need to accomplish your worthy objective. Moreover, your parish priest, your fellow instructors, the Church school director and the whole Church are by your side to support you, to answer your questions and to advise about all the things related to your duty.

The aim of this brief methodological guide is to help align with you and the rest of the Church school team on the key things which we do and the ones which we avoid. If we can find the common ground for the key things, all other things should follow and we believe so because this is what Jesus Christ has taught us – "seek first the kingdom of God and His righteousness, and all these things shall be added to you" (*Mt 6:33*). We are already aligned on the basic things, such as our faith – true and simple Orthodoxy. This guide takes this one step further to facilitate your work as a Church school instructor.

Teaching Philosophy

> "You are the salt of the earth (…) You
> are the light of the world" (*Mt 5:13, 15*).

The quote above is about true believers and it also applies to faithful Church school instructors and students. This entails that instructors are to be worthy of this calling by being a good example to their students. They should also help students develop their living faith to be worthy of their Christian calling too.

> "The mind is not a vessel to be filled, but
> a fire to be kindled" (*Plutarch*).

Mere knowledge is not enough to fully help students in their Orthodox Christian journey (although knowledge is a good thing). For example, it is not enough to know about the Ten Commandments or to memorize them, but it is quite useful to help students ponder over them: why they are given, how to fulfill them in real life situations, where to get help and so on. This works even in young student groups, although instead of a discussion, an alternative activity can be used to interact with a topic: brainstorming an idea (adjusted to the students' age), drawing a situation, asking to come up with students' own examples, etc.

> "I am the way, the truth, and the life"
> (*Jn 14:6*).

We see our students as little disciples of Christ who look to us to be educated about the Holy Trinity. We pray to the Lord to help us show to the children the True Way which they are to pursue – Jesus Christ, Who is our Wise Teacher, our Faithful and Loving Friend, our Saviour.

Why to Participate

"As iron sharpens iron, So a man sharpens the countenance of his friend" *(Pr 27:17)*.

Ukrainian Orthodox Church schools have a lot of benefits for the students who attend a Church school. However, students' parents, and sometimes even instructors, do not realize those although articulating these reasons may be a factor in bringing more students to Church schools. Therefore, this chapter addresses some of those reasons.

It is important for Christians not only to believe and practise their faith, but also to communicate with other fellow Christians, to learn from them, mutually support each other and accomplish even more than one can individually. A Church school is an excellent way to do just that as it allows students learn from their peers, discuss topic at their age level and even plan activities outside of the Church school (e.g. to participate in reading of the Epistle during a Church service). In fact, wise instructors and students' parents, too, often learn from students, be it their simplicity, sense of humour or other Orthodox Christian things.

Other reasons why parents may want to bring their children to a Ukrainian Orthodox Church school include:
- Church schools help families and the Church provide Orthodox education to their children – something that may serve a beacon in their everyday life;
- Ukrainian traditions (e.g. via carols) are explained;
- education is free and a certificate is issued to students after their successful completion of a course.

Volunteers

"God loves a cheerful giver" (2Cor 9:7).

Church schools are operable because of volunteers whose hearts the Lord has filled with love to glorify Him and to serve their neighbour in one of the most honourable ways of brining the Word of God to young minds and hearts through education. Church school instructors donate one of the most precious things that they have, their time, to serve the Lord and support their neighbour. This is the most important reason to volunteer.

Other reasons include the possibility to
- give back to the community;
- help and see students grow in their Orthodox faith;
- meet new people – fellow Orthodox Christian instructors;
- gain Canadian (volunteer) experience;
- obtain a reference letter to help grow career.

There are different ways to volunteer, including volunteering as:
- a Church school director;
- an instructor or teaching assistant (TA);
- a substitute instructor;
- a sports leader who prepares light workouts for students after the Liturgy and before their snack and lessons;
- a food manager who ensures that students have some healthy snacks after their workout and before their lessons.

Curriculum Considerations

The key purpose of Church school curriculum is to educate young people about:

- what it means to be a true Christian;
- how to rightly praise (*пра́вильно сла́вити*) the Lord in the Orthodox (*правосла́вна*) tradition;
- why we respect our neighbour not only within our closest, Canadian-Ukrainian community, but far beyond.

The Divine Liturgy (from Gr. *Λειτουργία*, "people work") is the primary service of the Church in which the faithful actively participate, a point which suggests that families should stick together and participate together. Consequently, Church school curriculum should be organized in such a way that promotes this liturgical unity and participation. The plan below meets this requirement and has been successfully put into practice:

- Church school begins right after the Divine Liturgy (after the Communion, but before any additional services, such as a memorial service (*панахи́да*));
- the school year is autumn through spring;
- classes are on Sundays and last about 60 minutes:
    - **15 minutes**: light physical exercises or an active game in the gym,
    - **5 minutes**: prayers before a meal and before a lesson (other prayers can be added as needed, for example, for an ill student, gratitude for recovery, etc.) followed by a light snack (in the classroom during the lesson),
    - **40 minutes**: the lesson in groups of similar age,

- o while students are at school, their parents are welcome to the Church hall where they can communicate with their fellow Orthodox Christians and have a snack.

To optimize curriculum, the following should be considered:
- 60 minutes are not enough for a lot, so lesson plans should be adapted accordingly; this, for example, is important in choosing and using any Church school Orthodox books as a lot of them are created for longer classes and, therefore, should be adjusted accordingly;
- the stress should be on the quality of knowledge:
  - o instead of covering as many topics as possible, pick the most important ones and study them in detail without haste,
  - o use abundant examples, if possible related to the modern world and students' everyday life,
  - o rather than explaining importance of something, ask the students to think about this and share their thoughts, which can then be completed with your own points,
  - o if possible, let students interact with information in different ways to remember it better and to make it more interesting for them; for example, instead of telling students about St. Paul's travels, show them the map or even make one with the students,
  - o to accommodate different learning styles and make lessons more interesting, activities can be diversified by singing carols, chanting prayers, making a tour of the Church, inviting "guests" (e.g. a parish priest or a choir director), etc.

A Lesson Plan Sample

The objective of this and any other Church school lesson is to help educate students in the true spirit of Orthodox Christian faith. Therefore, the plan below should be viewed as a guide, rather than a strict number of points to be covered or learned. This means that if students need additional time for any activity, quality discussion time should be granted rather than trying to pursue the plan. Moreover, the same lesson plan (even if it worked well the previous year) may need to be changed for a different group of students to accommodate the group size, students' age and their learning style.

In addition, lessons should vary in activity types, quantity of audiovisual aids, etc. to help improve dynamics of learning. Therefore, if the previous lessons were similar, the activities in this plan can be diversified.

Finally, Church school lesson plans, such as this one, should be linked to the practical aspect of students' life. Thus, if the specific examples from the parish life can be added to the plan instead of generic ones, those specific examples should be prioritized over the generic ones in this plan.

Plan

Topic:	**The Baptism of the Lord / Theophany / Epiphany / Feast of Jordan**
Duration:	*45 min.*
Aids:	The Bible, the icon of the feast
Alt. activities:	Prepare labels for holy water jars, prepare a to-do list for inviting a priest to bless home.

The Baptism of Christ

"It came to pass in those days that Jesus came from Nazareth of Galilee, and was baptized by John in the Jordan. And immediately, coming up from the water, He saw the heavens parting and the Spirit descending upon Him like a dove. Then a voice came from heaven, 'You are My beloved Son, in whom I am well pleased'" (*Mr 1:9-11*).

1. **Warm-up** (*5 min.*):
   - How are you today?
   - What feast did we celebrate on Dec. 25 (Jan. 7)?
   - Did you attend the service?
   - Were there many people in the Church?
   - Why do you think those people came?
     - o to worship with other faithful as a congregation (Church);
     - o to glorify the Lord;
     - o to cheerfully thank Him for all His gifts to us;
     - o to pray for Canada and Ukraine…

2. **Introduction to the new topic** (*5 min.*):
   - What are we going to celebrate on Jan. 6 (Jan. 19)?
     - o The Baptism of the Lord / Theophany / Epiphany / Feast of Jordan (*Хрещення Господнє / Богоявлення / Епіфанія / Йордан*).
   - Why is it called this way? What do you think happened on this day?
     - o On this day Jesus Christ, God the Son (*Бог-Син*) was baptized.
     - o From Gr. *Θεοφάνεια*, meaning "appearance of God" – God appeared to us.

3. **Bible reading by the students** (*5 min.*):
   - Find and read aloud *Mr 1:9-11*.
   - [for instructors only, here are the parallel places for reference: *Mt 3:13-16*; *Lk 3:21-22*; *Jn 1:29-34*].

4. **Icon discussion** (*5 min.*):
   - The instructor shows the icon of the Baptism of the Lord and asks the students to describe what they [do

12

not] see (if no icon can be found in as a hard copy option, it can be found on an electronic device (if possible, previously downloaded). Discussing the icon should facilitate the next activity.

5. **Bible discussion** (*10 min.*):
   - Who baptized Jesus Christ?
     - ○ John.
   - How do we call John?
     - ○ Saint John the Baptist (*Св. Іва́н Христи́тель*).
   - Who appeared in the bodily form of a dove when Jesus Christ was baptized?
     - ○ God the Holy Spirit (*Бог-Святи́й Дух*).
   - Whose voice did people hear when Jesus Christ was baptized?
     - ○ God the Father (*Бог-Оте́ць*).
   - How do we call God the Father, God the Son and God the Holy Spirit collectively?
     - ○ The Holy Trinity (*Свята́ Трі́йця*).
   - By the way, when we cross ourselves, how do we do this and what does it mean?
     - ○ We put our three fingers together and touch our forehead, right and then left shoulder and finally our stomach.
     - ○ We put our thumb, index and middle finger together, which symbolizes the Holy Trinity. We put our ring and little fingers pressed together against the palm symbolizing the two natures of Jesus Christ, His divinity and humanity.
   - So again, why is the feast of Baptism of the Lord also called Theophany?
     - ○ On this day the Holy Trinity appeared to us.

13

- What is the name of the river in which Jesus Christ was baptized?
  - The River Jordan.
- How do we greet each other on this feast?
  - Christ is baptized! (*Христо́с хреща́ється / хре́ститься / охрести́вся!*)
  - In the Jordan River / River Jordan! (*У рі́чці Йорда́ні!*)

6. **Linking the biblical story to the students' life** (*10 min.*):
- Who has a cross on the neck? Do you know when we usually receive our first cross?
  - A cross is given to a person (usually a baby) who is baptized in the Church. A cross is a symbol of Jesus Christ's victory over death; it is a symbol of us being Christians and it is also a symbol of facing and overcoming challenges in our lives: "(i)f anyone desires to come after Me, let him deny himself, and take up his cross, and follow Me." (*Mt 16:24*).
- Can anyone or just a priest baptize a person?
  - First of all, it should be mentioned that not only babies, but adults can be baptized (if they have never been baptized).
  - Generally speaking, only a priest (or a bishop) baptizes people.
  - In emergency situations (e.g. a high probability of death), any baptized Orthodox Christian can baptize another person by pouring water three times over that person's head or by this person's triple immersion into water saying: "The servant

of God [*NAME*] is baptized in the Name of the Father, Amen, and the Son, Amen, and the Holy Spirit, Amen."

- How many times does a person get baptized?
  - o Once. This is stated in the Creed: "I acknowledge one baptism for the remission of sins."
- Why do people baptize babies?
  - o Parents' responsibility is to provide bodily and spiritual nurture and to protect their babies.
- What do people do at Church for the feast of the Baptism of our Lord?
  - o People bring jars to the Church for the Great Blessing of Water (*Велúке Освя́чення Воdú*). The priest blesses the water and people take the holy water home to drink it with their families to help stay healthy and protected.
  - o Moreover, following this feast people invite the priest to bless their homes and the people therein.
- How do people prepare for the feast of Theophany?
  - o The day before the feast is a fast day. The feast day, however, is fast-free, even if it falls on Wednesday or Friday. By the way, the same fasting (and fast-free) rule applies to Christmas.
- Do you drink holy water sometimes? Why [not]?
- Does your family usually invite a priest to bless your home? Why [not]?

7. **Closing** (*5 min.*):
- Summary of the lesson.
- Announcing the topic for the next lesson.
- Praying together with the students.

Useful Resources

1. The **Bible**, New King James Version (NKJV):
   St Athanasius Orthodox Academy (2008). *The Orthodox Study Bible*. Nashville, TN: Thomas Nelson.

2. A free **Bible app** to read the Bible electronically (e.g. on a smartphone offline) in different languages:
   Riversoft Systems (2023). *MySword*. Retrieved January 23, 2023, from: https://www.mysword.info/download-mysword

3. **Different translations of the Bible** online:
   Online Parallel Bible Project (2023). *Bible hub*. Retrieved January 23, 2023, from: https://biblehub.com/

4. The **Ecumenical Patriarchate** official website in English:
   Retrieved January 23, 2023, from: https://ec-patr.org/en/home/

5. The **Ukrainian Orthodox Church of Canada** (UOCC) official website, including a brief history and Church's position on modern society's questions (*Home > Orthodox Faith > Beliefs and Practices*):
   Retrieved January 23, 2023, from: https://www.uocc.ca/

6. The **Orthodox Church of Ukrainian** (OCU) official website, including a brief history and Church calendar (*Home > Church > Calendar*):
   Retrieved January 23, 2023, from: https://www.pomisna.info/uk/

7. A **prayer book** in English and Ukrainian:
    Ukrainian Orthodox Church of Canada (2013). *'Good Shepherd' Prayer Book* (2nd ed.). Winnipeg, MB: Ecclesia Publishing Corporation.

8. **History** of the Ukrainian Orthodoxy:
    Огієнко, І. (1942). Українська Церква: *Нариси з історії Української Праовославної Церкви* (том 1). Прага: Видавництво Юрія Тищенко.

    Огієнко, І. (1942). Українська Церква: *Нариси з історії Української Праовославної Церкви* (том 2). Прага: Видавництво Юрія Тищенко.

9. A crowd-sourced **encyclopedia of Orthodoxy** (may be a good starting point for research):
    Orthodox Wiki (2023). Retrieved January 23, 2023, from: https://orthodoxwiki.org/Main_Page

10. The **UOCC Foundation**, – financial support for spiritual, educational and cultural projects:
    Retrieved January 23, 2023, from: https://www.uoccf.ca/

11. An **Orthodox Christian radio station**:
    Antiochian Orthodox Christian Archdiocese of North America (2023). *Ancient Faith Radio*. Retrieved January 23, 2023, from: https://www.ancientfaith.com/

12. **Inspirational poetry** on Orthodox topics:
    Wise, I. (2023). *Wise and Harmless Poetry*. Retrieved January 23, 2023, from https://wiseandharmlesspoetry.wordpress.com/

THE CHURCH
A Brief History

Orthodox Christianity is sometimes referred to as "ancient faith". Faith in Christ has been guiding (and is still doing so) faithful people to salvation since old times. Different places in the Bible, including the Old Testament – written BC (before Christ) – point to the Messiah. The very first chapter in the Bible describes creation of the world by God and uses the plural form "Let Us make…" (*Gen 1:26*), a linguistic feature indicating that God the Father is working with God the Son (Christ). Thus, Orthodox Christianity, can be said to be ancient, indeed.

The "official" birthday of the Church is Pentecost (*П'ятдеся́тниця*). Christ bade to His disciples to remain in Jerusalem till the day on which they would be endued with the Holy Spirit (*Lk 24:49*). It is on this, fiftieth, day after Christ's Resurrection (Pascha), that this happened. Here is how the Bible describes this:

> "When the Day of Pentecost had fully come, they were all with one accord in one place. And suddenly there came a sound from heaven, as of a rushing mighty wind, and it filled the whole house where they were sitting. Then there appeared to them divided tongues, as of fire, and one sat upon each of them. And they were all filled with the Holy Spirit and began to speak with other tongues, as the Spirit gave them utterance." (*Acts 2:1-4*).

Following this event, the Apostles and other disciples began actively preaching the Good News (Eng. *Gospel*, Gr. *Εὐαγγέλιον*, Ukr. *Єва́нгеліє*) in Jerusalem and other parts of the world. St. Andrew the Apostle (*Апо́стол Андрі́й Первозва́ний*),

Peter's brother, was the one who preached the Good News to the Scythians ['sɪθ i ənz] (*Скіфи*) on the territory of the present-day Ukraine. Besides St. Andrew, the Gospel was also spread by the Greeks, some of whom dwelled in the southern part of the present-day Ukraine. Thus, modern Ukrainians' ancestors accepted Christianity from one of the Apostles and some of the first Christians among the Greeks. This happened as early as the first century AD (anno Domini).

The Baptism of Rus', which happened in 988 AD is not the beginning of Christianity on our lands. It is rather a decisive transition from the time when Christianity was an "underground" religion to the time when it became the "mainstream" faith recognized at the state level. This was also the so-called civilizational choice of the society, the direction in which the generations of Ukrainians to come would follow.

The Church of the Tithes (*Десятинна Церква*) or Church of the Dormition of the Virgin in Kyiv was built around this period, namely from 989 and 996. Another Church that was built in Kyiv about the same period is Saint Sophia Cathedral (*Софія Київська*). It was built from 1011 to 1018 by Yaroslav (Iaroslav), the Grand Prince of Kyiv, known as Yaroslav the Wise (*Ярослав Мудрий*). This Church bears witness to the fact that once Christianity came to our land, it stayed there for good. Both these Churches are still one of the main attractions in the capital of Ukraine and Liturgies are still regularly served there.

The baptism of Rus' triggered creation of the Metropolis of Kyiv and all Rus'. The Metropolis of Kyiv and all Rus' was under the jurisdiction of the Ecumenical Patriarchate of Constantinople and the episcopal seat (cathedral) was in Kyiv.

The fact that the Metropolis of Kyiv and all Rus' was created under the jurisdiction of the Ecumenical Patriarchate meant that the Ukrainian Orthodox Church was recognized as early as 988.

It is by God's grace and through the Metropolis of Kyiv and all Rus' that Christianity began spreading further, including to the north, far beyond the territory of the present-day Ukraine. However, instead of gratitude and in the course of uncanonical (i.e. against the Orthodox Church rules) events, the Church of Ukraine was deprived of the means to maintain relationships with her mother Church in Constantinople. This required that the Ukrainian Church should resolve this, which, with God's help, happened successfully in both Canada and Ukraine.

The Ukrainians coming to Canada brought their Orthodox faith with them. A lot of Ukrainian Orthodox Churches were built in Canada, especially in Saskatchewan, Alberta and Manitoba. The UOCC was received into the Ecumenical Patriarchate in 1990.

The OCU became autocephalous (independent) in 2019. At that time different Orthodox Churches in Ukraine united into one Church. This Church was recognized with the patriarchal tomos and is in now commemorated (in the diptych) as an equal among other autocephalous Orthodox Churches.

The UOCC and the OCU are independent from each other and other Churches. The friendly relationships with other Churches are seen in that priests can participate in Lutrgies together, and the faithful can go to the Communion and partake in other Sacraments in other Orthodox Churches glorifying the Lord together, just as Jesus Christ's will about true believers is: "that they all may be one" (*Jn 17:21*).

The Holy Mysteries

The holy Mysteries or Sacraments (*Святі Таїнства*) are special actions by the Church through divine grace. They are called Mysteries because we believe the thing that we see to be something else. Generally, the faithful participate in seven Mysteries in the Church:

- **Communion** (or "Eucharist" – *Причáстя / Євхарúстія*) – the Orthodox Church understands Communion as having all things in common and sharing the same faith. Only those who are members of the Orthodox Church and who have prepared themselves through prayer, fasting and recent confession may participate in this Sacrament. The Church encourages her faithful to receive Communion (following the proper preparation) as often they can, if possible during every Liturgy after proper preparation. Communion is viewed by the Church as the centre of Christians' life in the Lord. The Eucharist was established by Jesus Christ and is described by the Bible (*Mt 26:26-28*);
- **Baptism** (*Хрéщення*);
- **Chrismation** [Confirmation] (*Миропомáзання [після Хрéщення]*);
- **Confession** (*Спóвідь [Покаяння]*);
- **Holy Unction** or Anointing of the Sick (*Єлеопомáзання [хвóрого], Миропомáзання або Соборувáння*);
- **Marriage** (*Вінчáння [шлюб]*);
- **Ordination** (*Хіротóнія [Священство]*).

Different Calendars and Pascha

Within the Ukrainian Orthodox community, there has been an "artificial" debate about which calendar is the most "Orthodox", the old one (Julian) or the new one (Revised Julian or Gregorian) and, consequently, which dates are to be used to, for example, celebrate Christmas, Dec. 25 or Jan. 7. The simple answer is that none of these calendars is more Orthodox than the other. Regardless of what calendar is used by a Church, feast days are celebrated on the same date. For example, all Churches (and, therefore, all Christians) celebrate Christmas on Dec. 25. The only difference is that depending on which calendar is used, this date may fall on Dec. 25 or Jan 7 according to the 'lay' calendar. Moreover, whenever a Church celebrates a feast day, such as Christmas, she does not celebrate a specific date, but the importance of and the meaning behind that date. For instance, the Church does know the exact date on which Jesus Christ was born, but what the faithful do know is that, truly, the Saviour came to save the human race and this is what they celebrate.

The calendar question is well described by the following poem:
Що ми святкуємо на Різдво

Точну дату Різдва хто знає?
Але важливе інше, а саме,
Що Господь про нас дбає,
Що через Христа людина на спасіння надію має.

Отож, що ми святкуємо?
Не дату, не календар,
Але те, що до Світла крокуємо;
Любов, надію, віру, що від Бога дістали даруємо.

Some Orthodox Churches have chosen to observe feast days according to the new style (e.g. the Orthodox Church of Greece, the Romanian Orthodox Church), whereas others use the old style (e.g. the Orthodox Church of Georgia). At the moment of publishing this book, the UOCC still uses the old style calendar, whereas, the OCU allows her faithful to celebrate Christmas, for example, based on either style, depending on the decision of the faithful at any given parish. Despite the different styles that Orthodox Churches use for Christmas and other feasts, they all celebrate Pascha on the same date (based on the Julian calendar).

Pascha is the most important Feast in the Church. Generally speaking, there are twelve most important feasts that are celebrated by the Orthodox Church, but Pascha is so important that it is not even a part of those twelve feasts. Pascha is all about the triumph of Light over darkness, eternal things over temporary ones, freedom over bondage, Life over death. Pascha is a movable feast. Below is how the date for celebrating Pascha is calculated:

- **Pascha** (Easter) [the Feast of Feasts] (*Пáсха, Велúкдень*) – the Resurrection of our Lord and Saviour Jesus Christ. The Feast is celebrated on the Sunday which follows the first full moon after the vernal (spring) equinox (when daytime and nighttime are of equal length), the actual beginning of spring. If the full moon happens to fall on a Sunday, Pascha is observed the following Sunday. The day taken by the Church to be the invariable date of the vernal equinox is Mar. 21.

Feasts

Below are Twelve Great Feasts (Gr. *Δωδεκάορτον*, Ukr. *Дванадесяті свята*), the old style dates are in brackets:

- The **Baptism of the Lord**, Theophany, Epiphany, Feast of Jordan (*Хрещення Господнє, Богоявлення, Водохреща, Йордан*) – Jan. 6 (Jan. 19);
- The **Presentation of Jesus at the Temple**, Candlemas (*Стрітення Господнє*) – Feb. 2 (Feb. 15);
- The **Annunciation** (*Благовіщення*) – Mar. 25 (Apr. 7);
- The **Entry into Jerusalem**, Willow / Palm Sunday (*Вхід Господній до Єрусалиму, Вербна неділя*) – the Sunday before Pascha;
- The **Ascension of Christ** (*Вознесіння Господнє*) – 40 days after Pascha;
- **Pentecost** (*П'ятдесятниця, День Святої Трійці День Зіслання Святого Духа, Зелена неділя*) – 50 days after Pascha;
- The **Transfiguration of Jesus** (*Преображення Господнє, Спас*) – Aug. 6 (Aug. 19);
- The **Dormition of the Theotokos** (*Успіння Пресвятої Богородиці*) – Aug. 15 (Aug. 28);
- The **Nativity of the Theotokos** (*Різдво Пресвятої Богородиці*) – Sept. 8 (Sept. 21);
- The **Elevation** / Exaltation **of the Cross** (*Воздвиження Хреста Господнього*) – Sept. 14 (Sept. 27);
- The **Presentation of the Theotokos** (*Введення до храму Пресвятої Богородиці*) – Nov. 21 (Dec. 4);
- **Christmas**, the Nativity of Christ (*Різдво Христове*) – Dec. 25 (Jan. 7).

Church Greetings

The faithful of the Ukrainian Orthodox Church around the world greet one another in a certain way based on whether it is a specific feast or regular day:

- The **Baptism of Christ** greeting:
  - Christ is baptized! (*Христóс хрещáється / хрéститься / охрестúвся!*)
  - In the Jordan River / River Jordan! (*У рíчці Йордáні!*)

- **Pascha** greeting:
  - Christ is risen! (*Христóс воскрéс!*)
  - Indeed He is risen! (*Воíстину воскрéс!*)

- **Christmas** greeting:
  - Christ is born! (*Христóс рождáється / народúвся!*)
  - [Let us] Glorify Him! (*Славíмо / славíте Йогó!*)

- **Everyday** Church greeting:
  - Glory be to Jesus Christ! (*Слáва Ісýсу Христý!*)
  - Glory be forever! (*Слáва навíки!*)

Fasts

Besides feasts, the Orthodox Church also blesses her faithful to observe fasts (*пости*). Fasts, however, are not the aim, but a means of achieving better Christian things, such as more attentive prayer, charity, endurance, etc. Fasting time can be an opportunity to help realign with the true values, such as faith, hope, love, joy and Christian daring. Fasting is intended to help the faithful and not to deprive them of anything useful for salvation. Fasting is meant to be helpful, but using it incorrectly (just as any tool or physical exercises) may not serve the faithful well. Therefore, the Church encourages her faithful to use fasting wisely, it permits relaxing the strictness of fasting in certain situations. As for Church school students, their families should help them make optimal decisions about fasting. For students' families, in turn, it may be a good idea to discuss their questions about fasting with their priest.

Below are the multi-day fasts that are observed by the Church:
- The **Great Lent** (*Великий піст*) – 40 days before Pascha; it is followed by the Holy Week (*Страсний тиждень*), during which fast is observed too.
- The **Apostles' Fast** (*Петрівка*) – is the period from the Monday after All Saints (the Sunday after Pentecost) to the feast day of Ss. Peter and Paul on Jun. 29 (Jul. 12).
- The **Dormition Fast** (*Спасівка*) – two weeks before the Feast of the Dormition of the Theotokos, i.e. Aug. 1 – 14 (Aug. 14 – 27).
- The **Nativity Fast**, Advent, St. Philip's Fast (*Різдвяний піст, Пилипівка*) – 40 days prior to Christmas, i.e. Nov. 15 – Dec. 24 (Nov. 28 – Jan. 6).

Additionally, the Orthodox Church provides opportunities to her faithful to fast on the following days:

- Eve of Theophany – Jan. 5 (Jan. 18).
- Beheading of St. John the Baptist – Aug. 29 (Sept. 11).
- Elevation of the Holy Cross – Sept. 14 (Sept. 27).
- Before Communion – from midnight till receiving Communion (the same day).
- Every Wednesday and Friday in remembrance of the betrayal of Christ and His Crucifixion.

If Theophany or Christmas are on Wednesday or Friday, there is no hast on those days. Additionally, there are several fast-free weeks without the usual fasting on Wednesdays and Fridays:

- Week following the Sunday of the Publican and Pharisee (*Неділя про митаря та фарисея*) – 1st week of the Lenten Triodion (*Тріódь*) or the 3rd week before the Great Lent.
- Bright Week, Pascha Week (*Світлий тиждень, Пасхáльний тиждень, Великóдній тиждень, Світла седмиця*) – the week following Pascha.
- Trinity Week – the week following Pentecost.
- Afterfeast (*віддáння свята*) of Christmas to Theophany Eve – Dec. 25 through Jan. 4 (Jan. 7 – 17).

There multiple places in the Bible, in which fasting is referenced. In the abstract below, for example, Jesus Christ explains to His followers how to fast:

"… when you fast, do not be like the hypocrites, with a sad countenance. For they disfigure their faces that they may appear to men to be fasting. Assuredly, I say to you, they have their reward. But you, when you fast, anoint your head and wash your face, so that you do not appear to men to be fasting, but to your Father who is in the secret place; and your Father who sees in secret will reward you openly" (*Mt 6:16-18*).

St. John Chrysostom points out that:

"(t)he value of fasting consists not only in avoiding certain foods, but in renouncing all sinful attitudes, thoughts and desires. (…) If you fast, let it show in your works! If you see a brother in need, take pity on him. If you see a brother being praised, do not be jealous. In order for fasting to be true, it cannot involve only fasting with the mouth; you must also fast with your eyes, ears, feet, hands and your whole body… You fast with your hands when you keep them pure through selfless service to others. You fast with your feet when you are swift to love and serve. You fast with your eyes when you do not look at impure things, or when you do not scrutinize others in order to criticize them. Fast from all that puts your soul and your holiness at risk. It would be useless to deprive your body of food, but to feed your heart with sordid things, with impurity, with egoism, with rivalries or with comforts. You fast from food, but you allow yourself to listen to many vain and worldly things. You should also fast with your ears. You should fast from listening to things that people say about your brothers and sisters, to lies about others, especially gossip, rumors or harsh words that harm others. Besides fasting with your mouth, you must fast by not saying anything that could harm anyone else. After all, **what good is it for you to abstain from meat if you devour your brother?**"

Presents and Carols

Presents and carols are two popular things that are associated with winter feasts. In the Ukrainian Orthodox tradition, people give presents, especially to children, on St. Nicholas Day, Dec. 6 (Dec. 19) in recognition of this Saint's acts of kindness. In some countries, such as Canada, it is common to share gifts for Christmas commemorating the fact that the three Wise Men brought their gifts to Baby Jesus (*Mt 2:11*). In some places (e.g. Greece), it is common to give presents for the New Year Day, the day on which the Church commemorates St. Basil the Great, who, among other things, is well known for his charitable acts. Regardless of when exactly one gives and receives presents, it may be a good idea to remind Church school students about the notion of charity, gratitude and that it is more blessed to give than to receive (*Acts 20:35*).

It is common for Christians in different parts of the world to sing carols for Christmas. In the Ukrainian Orthodox tradition, however, this practice is particularly brisk. Ukrainian Orthodox Christians of all ages and in different parts of Ukraine, Canada and around the world sing carols. Moreover, not only the Ukrainian faithful sing carols, they also create new ones regularly. In Churches, carols are usually heard on Christmas and for several days following Christmas.

Carols are a way to glorify God and share Christmas joy with others. Therefore, carol singing is a good way to spend time together and to preach Christ in an exciting way. This is why, helping Church school students to learn a carol (or even to write one) may be an excellent activity in preparation for Christmas. Several popular carols are provided below in this chapter.

Great Joy at Our Door

Great joy at our door, like never before
Has shined like a star for those at sea and ashore. }×2

The tidings that's merry today we carry,
Like a humble baby, Christ is born of the Virgin Mary. }×2

Angels are pronouncing peace, let songs not cease.
Let people's hearts be filled with hope and bliss. }×2

O Great God on high, we will praise You far and nigh.
Let the answer that we hear at Your Kingdom gate be "Aye!" }×2

Heaven and Earth

Heaven and earth, heaven and earth today are rejoicing,
Angels and people, angels and people jointly celebrating.

Christ is born and swaddled; God is embodied.
Angels are chanting, Wise Men contemplating,
Shepherds celebrating,
Wonder, wonder resonating.

In Bethlehem, in Bethlehem the joyous proclamation:
Mary – the Virgin, Mary – the Virgin gave birth to the Saviour.

Christ is born and swaddled; God is embodied.
Angels are chanting, Wise Men contemplating,
Shepherds celebrating,
Wonder, wonder resonating.

Нова́ ра́дість ста́ла

Нова́ ра́дість ста́ла, яка́ не бува́ла,
Над верте́пом зі́рка яскра́ва сві́ту засія́ла.   } ×2

Де Христо́с народи́вся, з Ді́ви воплоти́вся,
Як люди́на пелена́ми убо́го пови́вся.   } ×2

А́нгели співа́ють, сла́ву сповіща́ють,
Як на не́бі, так і на землі́ мир проповіда́ють.   } ×2

Дай нам ми́рно жи́ти, Тобі́ догоди́ти,
І з Тобо́ю в Твоі́м Ца́рстві по вік ві́ки жи́ти.   } ×2

Не́бо і земля́

Не́бо і земля́, небо і земля́ ни́ні торжеству́ють,
А́нгели й лю́ди, а́нгели й лю́ди ве́село святку́ють.

Христо́с народи́вся, Бог воплоти́вся,
А́нгели співа́ють, ца́рі віта́ють,
Покло́н відда́ють, па́стирі гра́ють,
Ди́во, ди́во повіда́ють.

У Вифлее́мі, у Вифлее́мі весе́ла нови́на́,
Пре́чи́ста Ді́ва, Пре́чи́ста Ді́ва народи́ла Си́на,

Христо́с народи́вся, Бог воплоти́вся,
А́нгели співа́ють, ца́рі віта́ють,
Покло́н відда́ють, па́стирі гра́ють,
Ди́во, ди́во повіда́ють.

31

God Eternal

God Eternal – is born, behold!
He came down from above
To save us with His love.   ×2
What a joy untold!

Bethlehem was His place of birth,
He is our Saviour and Lord;
Him we will glorify in one accord,   ×2
Our God among us on earth.

Glory to Jesus Christ evermore!
Praise to God from all of us
For all the things He does.   ×2
Come, let us adore.

Glory to God in the highest, And on earth peace, goodwill toward men! (*Lk 2:14*)

He [Jesus Christ] Himself is our peace… (*Eph 2:14*)

Rejoice in the Lord always. Again I will say, rejoice! (*Php 4:4*)

…with God all things are possible. (*Mt 19:26*)

And now abide faith, hope, love, these three; but the greatest of these is love. (*1Cor 13:13*)

Бог Предві́чний

Бог Предві́чний народи́вся!
Прийшо́в днесь із небе́с,
Щоб спасти́ люд Свій ввесь,
І ут́шився.

×2

У Вифлеє́мі народи́вся, –
Госпо́дь наш, Христо́с наш
І Спас наш для всіх нас
Нам народи́вся.

×2

«Сла́ва Бо́гу» заспіва́ймо!
Честь Си́ну́ Бо́жому́,
Господе́ві на́шому,
Поклі́н відда́ймо.

×2

Prayers

The Lord's Prayer

Our Father, who art in heaven, hallowed be Thy Name. Thy Kingdom come. Thy Will be done, on earth as it is in heaven. Give us this day our daily bread and forgive us our trespasses as we forgive those who trespass against us. And lead us not into temptation, but deliver us from the evil one. Amen.

Prayer Before Lessons 1

Most gracious Lord, send down upon us the grace of Your Holy Spirit to grant us intelligence and strengthen our spiritual powers that we may be attentive to our studies and grow up to glorify You, our Creator, to the joy of our parents and the benefit of our Church and people.

Prayer Before Lessons 2
(Prayer to the Holy Spirit)

O Heavenly King, Comforter, the Spirit of truth, everywhere present and filling all things, Treasury of blessings and Giver-of-life, come and dwell in us, and cleanse us from every impurity, and save our souls, o Good One.

Prayer After Lessons 1

We thank You, our Creator, for having granted us Your Grace to be attentive to this instruction. Bless our instructors and parents, who lead us to the knowledge of good. Grant us the intelligence and strength to persevere in our studies. Amen.

Молитви

Отче наш (Господня молитва)

Отче наш, що єси на небесах, нехай святиться Ім'я Твоє; нехай прийде Царство Твоє; нехай буде воля Твоя, як на небі, так і на землі. Хліб наш насущний дай нам сьогодні; і прости нам провини наші, як і ми прощаємо винуватцям нашим; і не введи нас у спокусу, але визволи нас від лукавого. Амінь.

Молитва перед навчанням 1

Милосердний Господи, пошли нам благодать Духа Твого Святого, що подає розум і зміцнює духовні сили наші, щоб ми, уважно переймаючи науку, виросли Тобі, Творцеві нашому, на славу, батькам нашим на радість, Церкві та народу нашому на користь. Амінь.

Молитва перед навчанням 2
(молитва до Святого Духа)

Царю Небесний, Утішителю, Духу істини, що всюди єси та все наповняєш, Скарбе добра і життя Подателю, прийди і вселися в нас, і очисти нас від усякої скверни, і спаси, Благий, душі наші.

Молитва після навчання 1

Дякуємо Тобі, Боже, Творцеві нашому, що Ти сподобив нас ласки Твоєї розуміти навчання. Благослови наших викладачів і батьків, які ведуть нас до пізнання добра. Пошли нам розум і силу продовжувати науку нашу. Амінь.

Prayer After Lessons 2
(Prayer to the Most Holy Theotokos)
It is truly worthy to bless You, o Theotokos, Ever-blessed, Most Pure and the Mother of our God. More honourable than the Cherubim and more glorious beyond compare than the Seraphim, without corruption You gave birth to God the Word. True Theotokos, we magnify You.

Prayer Before a Meal 1
(After the "Lord's Prayer")
O Lord, the eyes of all look to You with hope. You give food to all in due season. You open Your generous hand and You fill every living thing with Your favour. Amen.

Prayer Before a Meal 2
O Lord, Jesus Christ, Son of God, you blessed the food of Your disciples. Bless also this food, for we believe in You, we hope in You, we pray to You and we glorify You, unto the ages of ages. Amen.

Prayer After a Meal
O Christ our God, we give thanks to You, for You have satisfied us with Your earthly blessings. Deprive us not of Your heavenly Kingdom. O Saviour, as You came in the midst of Your disciples, and gave them peace, so come to us and save us. Amen.

Молитва після навчання 2
(похвала́ Пресвяті́й Богоро́диці)

Досто́йно є, і це є і́стина, сла́вити Тебе́, Богоро́дицю, Присноблаже́нну і Пренепоро́чну, і Ма́тір Бо́га на́шого. Чесні́шу від херуви́мів і незрівня́нно славні́шу від серафи́мів, що без істлі́ння Бо́га-Сло́во народи́ла, су́щу Богоро́дицю, Тебе́ велича́ємо.

Молитва пе́ред ї́жею 1
(Після «О́тче наш»)

Го́споди, о́чі всіх до Те́бе зверта́ються із наді́єю. Ти дає́ш пожи́ву всім своєча́сно. Ти простяга́єш ще́дру ру́ку Твою́ і наповня́єш усі́х благоволі́нням Свої́м. Амі́нь.

Молитва пе́ред ї́жею 2

Го́споди, Ісу́се Хри́сте, Си́ну Бо́жий, Ти благослови́в стра́ви Свої́м ученика́м, благослови́ ж і нам пожи́ву цю, бо і ми у Те́бе ві́руємо, сподіва́ємося на Те́бе, Тобі́ мо́лимося та Те́бе прославля́ємо на ві́ки вікі́в. Амі́нь.

Молитва після ї́жі

Хри́сте Бо́же наш, дя́куємо Тобі́, що Ти наси́тив нас земни́ми Твої́ми дара́ми. Не позба́в нас і Небе́сного Твого́ Ца́рства, але́ як прийшо́в Ти, Спа́се, по́між учеників Свої́х і мир дав їм, прийди́ до нас і спаси́ нас. Амі́нь.

Prayer For Healing

Jesus Christ, Healer of our souls and bodies, look with Your merciful eyes at Your servants (*their names*) who are sick. Hearken to our sincere supplications and grant Your servants relief and healing so that they may serve You and vouchsafe them the Kingdom of God that together with Your saints they may glorify You, the Loving Lord, with the Father and the Holy Spirit, now and ever and unto the ages of ages. Amen.

Prayer of Gratitude

We thank You, o Lord, for everyone and everything; for what happened and from what You saved us; for all the good things, which we know and for the ones which we do not know, which are even more. We believe that You are not only near, but also love us and take care of us and guide us to salvation.

We thank You for air, water, food, clothing, and home. Thank You for our relatives and neighbours; for the Church, for our Motherland, for our families. Thank You for life, health, light, sight and all our feelings. Thank You for education, work and rest. Thank You for the just peace and for our mother tongue.

(we can add all for which we are sincerely grateful to God)

Lord, let Your servants, remembering all Your bounties and favours, glorify You in thought, word, and deed, and let them, like bright lights, shine to others. Glory to the Father, and to the Son, and to the Holy Spirit, now and ever and unto the ages of ages. Amen.

Моли́тва за оду́жання

Ісу́се Хри́сте, Лі́карю душ і тіл на́ших, погля́нь милосе́рдним о́ком Своїм на рабі́в Твоїх (*імена́*), які́ нездужа́ють. Прихили́сь до щи́рих блага́нь на́ших, пода́й полегшення та зці́лення від неду́ги раба́м Твоїм, щоб вони́ послужи́ли Тобі́ та сподо́би їх Твого́ Ца́рства Небе́сного, щоб ра́зом зі святи́ми Твоїми, сла́вили Тебе́, Го́спода Лю́блячого, з Отце́м і Святи́м Ду́хом за́вжди, ни́ні, і повсякча́с, і на ві́ки вікі́в. Амі́нь.

Подя́чна моли́тва

Дя́куємо Тобі́, Го́споди, за всіх і за все; за те, що ста́лося і за те, від чо́го вбері́г Ти нас; за все добро́, про яке́ ми зна́ємо і за те, про яке́ ми не зна́ємо, якого́ ще бі́льше. Ві́руємо, що Ти не ті́льки по́руч, але́ й лю́биш нас і дба́єш і до спасі́ння веде́ш.

Дя́куємо Тобі́ за пові́тря, во́ду, їжу, о́дяг, житло́. Дя́куємо за рі́дних на́ших і бли́жніх; за Це́ркву, за Батьківщи́ну, за на́ші роди́ни. Дя́куємо за життя́, здоро́в'я, сві́тло, зір і всі на́ші відчуття́. Дя́куємо за навча́ння, робо́ту та відпочи́нок. Дя́куємо за справедли́вий мир і за на́шу рі́дну мо́ву.

(Мо́жна дода́ти все те, за що ми щи́ро вдя́чні Бо́гу.)

Го́споди, неха́й раби́ Твої пам'та́ючи про всі щедро́ти та ла́ски Твої сла́влять Тебе́ у ду́мці, сло́ві, спра́ві та неха́й, як во́гники сві́тла, ся́ють й і́ншим. Сла́ва Отцю́, і Си́ну, і Свято́му Ду́хові, і ни́ні, і повсякча́с, і на ві́ки вікі́в! Амі́нь.

Prayer For the Departed

O Lord, forgive the sins of Your departed servants (*their names*). Establish their souls where the righteous repose and make their memory to be eternal.

(Here we can read "The Lord's Prayer".)

The Symbol Of Faith (The Creed)

I believe in one God, the Father, Almighty, Creator of heaven and earth and of all things visible and invisible.

And in one Lord, Jesus Christ, the Only-begotten Son of God, begotten of the Father before all ages. Light of Light, true God of true God, begotten, not created, being of one essence with the Father, by Whom all things were made. Who for us men and for our salvation came down from the heavens and was incarnate of the Holy Spirit and the Virgin Mary and became man. Who was crucified for us under Pontius Pilate and suffered and was buried. And He rose on the third day according to the Scriptures. And ascended into heaven and sits at the right hand of the Father. And He will come again with glory to judge the living and the dead; and His Kingdom will have no end.

And in the Holy Spirit, the Lord, the Giver-of-life, Who proceeds from the Father, Who together with the Father and the Son is worshipped and glorified, Who spoke through the prophets.

In One, Holy, Catholic and Apostolic Church. I acknowledge one baptism for the remission of sins. I await the resurrection of the dead and the life of the age to come. Amen.

Моли́тва за спочи́лих

Пода́й, Го́споди, відпу́щення гріхі́в спочи́лим раба́м Твоі́м (*імена́*). Посили́ ду́ши їх там, де пра́ведні Твоі́ спочива́ють і сотвори́ їм ві́чну па́м'ять.

(Да́лі мо́жна прочита́ти «О́тче наш»)

Си́мвол ві́ри

Ві́рую в Єди́ного Бо́га – Отця́, Вседержи́теля, Творця́ не́ба і землі́, всього́ ви́димого і неви́димого.

І в Єди́ного Го́спода Ісу́са Христа́, Си́на Бо́жого, Єдиноро́дного, від Отця́ ро́дженого пе́рше всіх віків. Сві́тло від Сві́тла, Бо́га Іс́тинного від Бо́га Іс́тинного, ро́дженого, нество́реного, єдиносу́щного з Отце́м, че́рез Котро́го все ста́лося. Він для нас, люде́й, і ра́ди на́шого спасі́ння зійшо́в з небе́с, і воплоти́вся від Ду́ха Свято́го і Марі́ї Ді́ви, і став люди́ною. І розп'я́тий був за нас при По́нтії Пила́ті, і стражда́в, і був похо́ваний. І воскре́с на тре́тій день, як було́ напи́сано. І вознісся на не́бо, і сиди́ть право́руч Отця́. І зно́ву при́йде у сла́ві суди́ти живи́х і ме́ртвих, і Ца́рству Йо́го не бу́де кінця́.

І в Ду́ха Свято́го, Го́спода Животво́рчого, що від Отця́ похо́дить, що Йому́ з Отце́м і Си́ном одна́кове поклоні́ння і одна́кова сла́ва, що говори́в че́рез проро́ків.

В Єди́ну, Свя́ту, Собо́рну і Апо́стольську Це́ркву. Визнаю́ одне́ хре́щення на відпу́щення гріхі́в. Чека́ю воскресі́ння ме́ртвих і життя́ бу́дучого ві́ку. Амі́нь.

Prayer For Ukraine (O Great and Only God)

(The spiritual anthem of Ukraine)

O Great and Only God, Safeguard our Ukraine,
Enlighten her with the rays of freedom and light.
Enlighten us, children, with the light of learning and knowledge;
O God, raise us in pure love for the Land.

We pray, o Only God, safeguard our Ukraine;
Bestow on Your people Your great mercy and grace.
Give us freedom, give us luck, give us good world, happiness;
Give, o God, to Your people many and many years.

Prayer For Victory

Almighty Lord, hearken to Your children's prayers, look at our
country at the time of the great tribulations. Bless and strengthen
our warriors, civil authorities, volunteers, medical workers,
Church and all the people who are resisting the insidious
aggressor on land, at sea and in the air. O Truth-loving Lord, do
not let our enemies destroy our people, country and all that is
holy.

We beseech You, give us victory with Your Name and make
just peace reign soon. Send the formidable leader of Your
Heavenly Host – the Archangel Michael – to help our brave
defenders to defeat the aggressor's devilish plans and to protect
our Motherland.

For Yours it is to have mercy on us and save us, o our God and
unto You we send up glory: to the Father and to the Son and to
the Holy Spirit, now and ever and unto the ages of ages. Amen.

Моли́тва за Украї́ну (Бо́же Вели́кий Єди́ний)

(Духо́вний гімн Украї́ни)

Бо́же Вели́кий Єди́ний, нам Украї́ну храни́,
Во́лі і сві́ту промі́нням Ти її осіни́.
Сві́тлом нау́ки і знання́ нас усі́х просвіти́,
В чи́стій любо́ві до кра́ю Ти нас, Бо́же, зрости́.

Мо́лимось, Бо́же Єди́ний, нам Украї́ну храни́,
Всі Свої́ ла́ски, щедро́ти Ти на люд Свій зверни́.
Дай йому́ во́лю, дай йому́ до́лю,
Дай, Бо́же, наро́ду мно́гая, мно́гая літа́.

Моли́тва за перемо́гу

Всеси́льний Го́споди, почу́й молитви́ діте́й Твої́х, споглянь в час важки́х ви́пробувань на держа́ву на́шу. Благослови́ та зміцни́ во́їнів на́ших, вла́ду, волонте́рів, меди́чних працівникі́в, Це́ркву та весь наро́д наш, які́ протистоя́ть підсту́пному агре́сору на землі́, на мо́рі й у пові́трі. Правдолюби́вий Го́споди, не дай ворога́м зни́щити наро́д, держа́ву та святи́ні на́ші.

Блага́ємо Тебе́, дару́й нам з І́менем Твої́м перемо́гу та справедли́вий мир набли́зь. Пошли́ грі́зного очі́льника небе́сного во́їнства Твого́ – архістрати́га Михаї́ла, на допомо́гу му́жнім захисника́м на́шим, щоб дия́вольські за́думи агре́сора зруйнува́ли вони́ та вберегли́ на́шу Батьківщи́ну.

Твоє́ бо є, щоб ми́лувати і спаса́ти нас, Бо́же наш, і Тобі́ сла́ву возсила́ємо, Отцю́, і Си́ну, і Свято́му Ду́ху, ни́ні і повсякча́с і на ві́ки вікі́в. Амі́нь.

God's Ten Commandments

1. I am the Lord, your God! You shall have <u>no other gods before Me</u>.

2. You shall <u>not make unto yourself any graven image</u>, or fashion the likeness of anything that is in heaven above, or that is on earth below, or that is in the waters under the earth: you shall not bow down to them nor worship them. For I am the Lord your God.

3. You shall <u>not take the name of the Lord your God in vain</u>.

4. Remember <u>the Sabbath day</u>, to keep it holy: six days you shall labour, and do all the work you have to do. But the seventh day is a Sabbath of the Lord your God.

5. <u>Honour your father and your mother</u>, that it may be well with you and that your days may be long upon the earth.

6. You shall <u>not murder</u>.

7. You shall <u>not commit adultery</u>.

8. You shall <u>not steal</u>.

9. You shall <u>not bear false witness</u> against your neighbour.

10. You shall <u>not covet</u> your neighbour's wife, you shall not covet your neighbour's house, nor his manservant, nor his maidservant, nor his ox, nor his ass, nor any of his cattle, nor anything that is your neighbour's.

Дéсять Зáповідей Божих

1. Я є Госпóдь Бог твій, нехáй не бýде тобí íнших богíв, крім Мéне!

2. Не твори собí кумѝра і всякого подíбного з тóго, що на нéбі вгорí, абó на землí внизý, і що у водí, під землéю. Не поклоняйся їм і не слýжи їм, бо Я Госпóдь Бог твій.

3. Не згáдуй íмені Гóспода, Бóга твогó, дарéмно.

4. Пам'ятáй день субóтній, щоб святѝти йогó: шість днів працюй і викóнуй у них всю прáцю свою, а день сьóмий субóта, для Гóспода Бóга твогó.

5. Шанýй бáтька твогó і мáтір твою, і дóбре тобí бýде і дóвго на землí жѝтимеш.

6. Не вбивáй.

7. Не чинѝ перéлюбу.

8. Не крадѝ.

9. Не свíдчи неправдѝво прóти блѝжнього твогó.

10. Не жадáй дружѝни блѝжнього твогó, не жадáй дóму блѝжнього твогó, áні раба йогó, áні рабѝні йогó, áні вола йогó, áні ослá йогó, áні всякої худóби йогó, áні всьóго, що у блѝжнього твогó.

45

Christian Virtues and Acts of Mercy

Virtues:
- Faith.
- Hope.
- Love.
- Wisdom.
- Justice.
- Patience.
- Moderation (temperance).

The seven acts of corporal mercy:
1. To feed the hungry.
2. To give drink to the thirsty.
3. To clothe the naked.
4. To receive the traveller.
5. To visit the sick.
6. To visit the imprisoned.
7. To bury the dead.

The seven acts of spiritual mercy:
1. To convert sinners to the path of righteousness.
2. To instruct the ignorant and help them to discern truth.
3. To give good counsel to your neighbour.
4. To comfort the sorrowful.
5. To bear personal wrongs patiently.
6. To sincerely forgive those who offend us.
7. To pray for the living and the dead.

Християнські чесноти та справи милосердя

Чесноти:
- Віра.
- Надія.
- Любо́в.
- Му́дрість.
- Справедли́вість.
- Терпели́вість.
- Стри́маність.

Сім справ тілесного милосе́рдя:
1. Голо́дного нагодува́ти.
2. Спра́глого напо́їти.
3. Наго́го одягну́ти.
4. Подоро́жнього прийня́ти.
5. Неду́жого відві́дати.
6. Ув'я́зненого відві́дати.
7. Поме́рлого похова́ти.

Сім справ духо́вного милосе́рдя:
1. Гра́шника настанови́ти на сте́жку пра́ведности.
2. Нерозу́много навчи́ти і допомогти́ пізна́ти пра́вду.
3. Бли́жньому, яки́й вага́ється до́бру пора́ду да́ти.
4. Засму́ченого вті́шити.
5. Особи́сту кри́вду терпля́че зно́сити.
6. Заподі́яну кри́вду щиросе́рдо проща́ти.
7. За живи́х і ме́ртвих моли́тися.

REFERENCES

1. The "Що ми святкуємо на Різдво" poem is from Wise and Harmless Poetry blog:
   Wise, I. (2023). *Що ми святкуємо на Різдво*. Wise and Harmless Poetry. Retrieved January 23, 2023, from https://wiseandharmlesspoetry.wordpress.com/2018/12/2 4/what-we-celebrate-at-christmas/

2. Most prayers in this book (except "Prayer For Healing", "Prayer For the Departed", "Prayer of Gratitude", "O Great and Only God" and "Prayer For Victory") are based on:
   Ukrainian Orthodox Church of Canada (2013). *'Good Shepherd' Prayer Book* (2nd ed.). Winnipeg, MB: Ecclesia Publishing Corporation.

3. The Ukrainian version of "O Great and Only God" is based on Olexander Koshetz's edition.

4. The Ukrainian version of the prayer for victory is based on:
   Православна Церква України (2023). *Молитва за перемогу України над агресором*. Retrieved January 23, 2023, from https://www.pomisna.info/uk/vsi-novyny/molytva-za-peremogu-ukrayiny-nad-agresorom/

5. The musical notes (in the "Carols / Колядки" section) are based on:
   При ватрі (2023). *Бог предвічний*. Retrieved January 23, 2023, from https://pryvatri.de/koladky/14-boh-predvichnyi

ST. PAUL'S MISSIONARY JOURNEYS

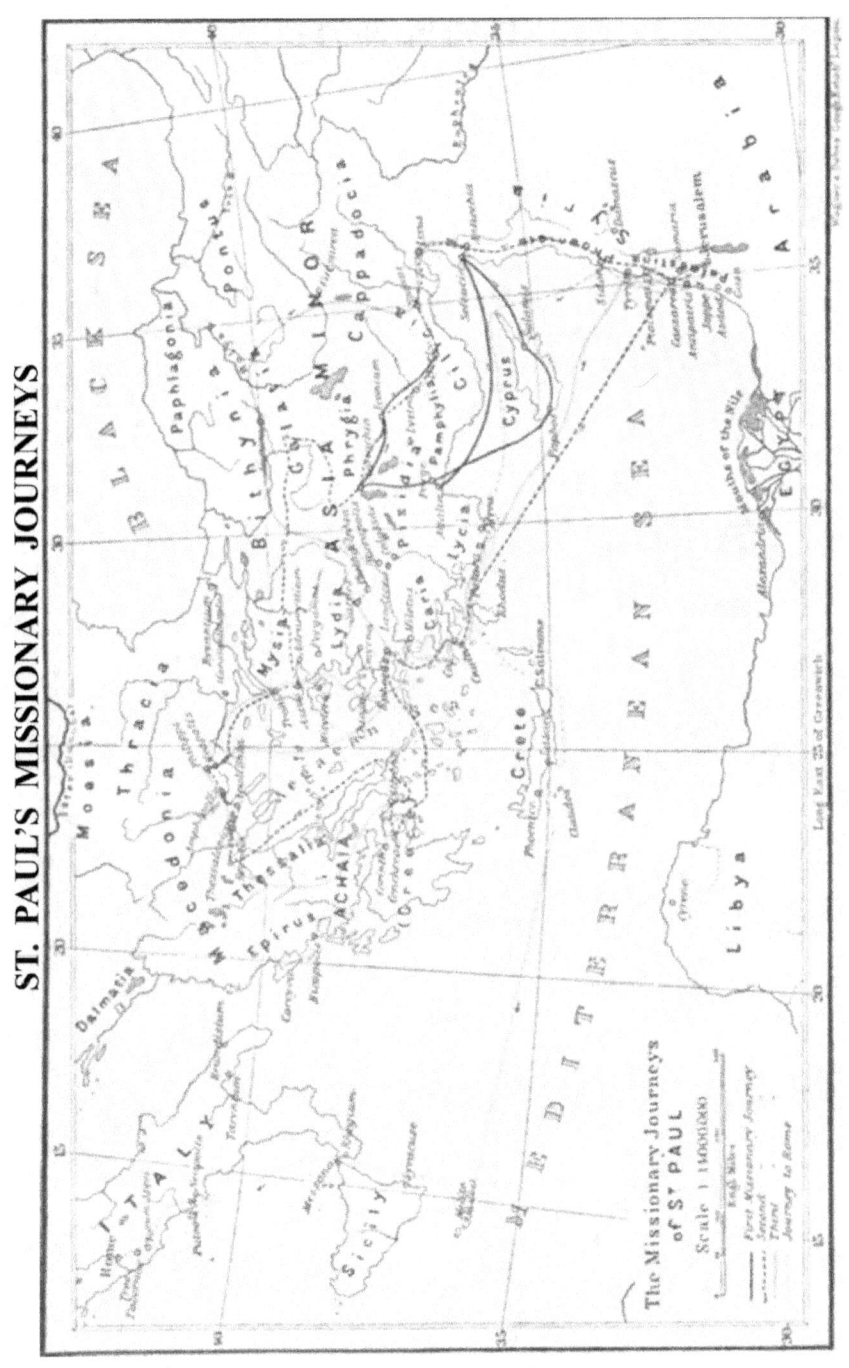

The Missionary Journeys
of St PAUL

Scale 1 16500000

First Missionary Journey
Second
Third
Journey to Rome

49

READER'S NOTES